ARLINGTON NATIONAL CEMETERY

ARLINGTON NATIONAL CEMETERY

DILLON PRESS
New York

Maxwell Macmillan Canada
Toronto

Maxwell Macmillan International
New York Oxford Singapore Sydney

By Catherine Reef

Photographic Acknowledgments

Photographs have been reproduced through the courtesy of Kendrick Photography (p. 9, 15, 20, 21, 36, 40, 42, 62); John W. Reef; National Gallery of Art; Library of Congress; Chester Simpson; National Portrait Gallery; National Aeronautics and Space Administration; and Don Sutherland. Cover photograph courtesy of John W. Reef.

Library of Congress Cataloging-in-Publication Data

Reef, Catherine.
    Arlington National Cemetery / Catherine Reef.
       p.   cm. — (Places in American history)
    Includes bibliographical references and index.
    Summary: Examines the history and current activities of the national burial place and shrine in Arlington, Virginia.
    ISBN 0-87518-471-5
    1. Arlington National Cemetery (Va.)—Juvenile literature.
    [1. Arlington National Cemetery (Va.)]   I. Title.   II. Series.
    F234.A7R44   1991
    975.5′295—dc20   91-17183

Dillon Press
Macmillan Publishing Company
866 Third Avenue
New York, NY 10022

Maxwell Macmillan Canada, Inc.
1200 Eglinton Avenue East
Suite 200
Don Mills, Ontario M3C 3N1

Macmillan Publishing Company is part of the Maxwell Communication Group of Companies.

First edition
Printed in the United States of America
10   9   8   7   6   5   4   3   2   1

CONTENTS

PLACES IN AMERICAN HISTORY

Arlington
National Cemetery

Ord 8 Weitzel Drive

Custis Walk

To Washington

President Taft's Grave

Memorial Gate

Memorial Drive

Visitors' Center

Jefferson Davis Highway

Arlington House

President J.F. Kennedy's Grave

N

U.S.S. Maine Memorial

Challenger Monument

Tomb of the Unknowns

Grant Drive

Roosevelt Drive

Eisenhower Drive

Memorial Drive

Confederate Monument

Memorial Amphitheater

Patton Drive

Washington, D.C.

VIRGINIA

Arlington National Cemetary

CHAPTER 1

THE NATION'S MOST IMPORTANT SHRINE

Heavy winds churned up the Pacific Ocean in February 1945. In calmer weather, the United States Marines could have easily anchored their landing boats near the tiny Japanese island of Iwo Jima. Now, rough waves pushed some of the boats up onto the beach and filled others with water. The waves washed pieces of equipment overboard.

At last the Marines made it ashore. The invasion of Iwo Jima had begun. The men dove onto the gray beaches for cover. Gunfire sounded all around them. In the hills up ahead, protected in deep trenches, was the enemy, Japanese soldiers. The Marines had little protection against the mortar shells—metal cases filled with explosives—landing nearby. An exploding mortar shell could scatter sharp pieces of metal over a wide area, burning and tearing human flesh.

The soldiers knew what they were up against. They had prepared for this battle for six months—and their goal was to capture the island of Iwo Jima.

It was World War II, and in the islands of the Pacific Ocean, the Americans were fighting against the Japanese. The Japanese used the airfield on Iwo Jima, which was just 660 miles (1,061 kilometers) from Japan, as a base for bombing raids all over the area. The Marines planned to take over the island and cut off this source of attack. Then American bomber pilots would be able to use the base to attack Japan. This would help bring the war to an end.

The battle lasted for almost a month. In the midst of the fighting, six Marines struggled to the top of Mount Suribachi, the highest point on the island. They set an American flag atop the

The United States Marine Corps Memorial is a statue of the six Marines who raised the American flag at Iwo Jima.

mountain. Seeing the flag gave the rest of the Marines the courage and strength they needed to win the difficult battle.

Today, three of the Marines who raised the flag at Iwo Jima are among the many heroes buried at Arlington National Cemetery. Outside the cemetery's gates stands a statue of all six Marines planting the flagpole in Iwo Jima's soil. Known as the United States Marine Corps Memorial, this statue honors the thousands of Marines who, over the years, have given their time—and often their lives—for their country.

Arlington National Cemetery is located in Arlington, Virginia, across the Potomac River from Washington, D.C. It is America's greatest national shrine—a place treated with special respect because of its historic importance.

More than two hundred thousand men, women, and children are buried in Arlington's 612 acres (247.9 hectares). Many are famous people, such as presidents, military leaders,

Supreme Court judges, and astronauts. Other people buried at Arlington are known only to their friends and relations. Most are veterans of war—people who fought for the United States. Some of those buried at Arlington are unknown. They, too, died in war, but their bodies could not be identified.

Every year, four million people visit Arlington's graves and memorials. They come to honor these brave men and women and the important work that they did. The visitors come from all over the United States and from countries throughout the world. They include school groups on field trips, families with young children, retired men and women, and soldiers and sailors in uniform. Political leaders from other countries who are visiting the president often come to lay wreaths at different gravesites. Tour guides who speak their languages tell them about the history of Arlington.

As visitors approach the cemetery, they look

upon a pretty and peaceful scene. A stone-col-
umned mansion sits at the top of a hill. It is
Arlington House, once the home of Robert E.
Lee. Lee commanded the Confederate, or Southern, troops during the Civil War. Rolling lawns
and grand shaded trees surround the house. As
the hill slopes downward, visitors can see white
marble tombstones that cover the grass. They
spread out in all directions, in row after row,
almost as far as the eye can see. Most are the
same size and shape, and each marks a grave.

Many of the tourists who come to Arlington
National Cemetery crowd around its best-known
sites. People often fill the space around President John F. Kennedy's grave. The Tomb of the
Unknowns attracts many visitors, too. The unknown soldiers buried there represent all Americans who died in wars and whose bodies were
never identified. People also visit a number of
memorials to important events and people in
American history. These include memorials to

Visitors climb the steps to Arlington House,
a mansion that once belonged to Robert E. Lee.

the astronauts who died aboard the space shuttle *Challenger* and the many nurses who cared for wounded soldiers during wartime. The memorials single out different people or events that helped shape the United States.

People often climb to Arlington's hilltop to tour Arlington House. This old home has been restored to look as it did when General Robert E. Lee, his wife, and their seven children lived there. Inside, tour guides inform visitors about Arlington's history and the life of General Lee. Looking out from the porch of Arlington House, visitors enjoy a beautiful view of the nation's capital. When President Kennedy saw that view in the 1960s, he said, "I could stay here forever."

Several times each year, there are services held in Arlington's Memorial Amphitheater that honor those who died serving their country. The biggest gatherings take place on Memorial Day and Veteran's Day, when up to five thousand people fill the amphitheater. Smaller, more

The view of Washington, D.C. from Arlington National Cemetery.

private ceremonies are held during the week at a chapel in Fort Myers, which is just outside of Arlington's chapel gate. After these services, the little-known heroes are laid to rest in the cemetery.

Arlington is a military cemetery, and many of the people buried there had outstanding military careers or died on active duty. Some members of their families may be buried at Arlington, too. Soldiers from almost every war America waged are buried there, from the Revolutionary War for independence to the Gulf War of 1991.

Each of Arlington's memorials tells a story. Together, they give visitors a picture of American history. And it all began with President George Washington's adopted grandson, George Washington Parke Custis.

FROM HOME TO BURIAL GROUND

To George Washington Parke Custis, President George Washington was both father and teacher. Washington told young Custis stories about the Revolutionary War and how he had led the American fight for independence from England. He taught the boy about farming and politics. Custis watched and listened as Washington met with important people, and he learned to admire Washington's honesty and fairness. The first president was really Custis's stepgrandfather. But George and Martha Washington had taken Custis and his sister in as young children, after their real father died in 1781. George and Martha raised the children at Mount Vernon, their home in Virginia.

The Washington family in 1796. George and Martha Washington are seated at the table. Young George Washington Parke Custis and his older sister are standing.

George Washington died when Custis was a young man. In his grief, Custis decided to create a memorial to Washington, the greatest man he had ever known. In 1802, he began to build an estate on a Virginia hilltop near Washington, D.C. This would become known as Arlington House, which is in Arlington National Cemetery. Custis gathered many items from Washington's life and career. He collected papers, clothing, battle flags—even the tent that Washington used at Yorktown, the battle that had ended the Revolutionary War. Custis had the collection together before he even finished Arlington House.

Custis had an "open door" policy, which meant that anyone interested in George Washington could visit. People who wanted to honor the first president came. Among the visitors were local farmers, residents of Washington, D.C., American presidents, and politicians from other countries. One of Custis's guests was the Marquis de Lafayette, a French nobleman. Lafayette had been friends with Washington and had fought with him during the Revolutionary War.

Custis hoped to raise a family at Arlington. He married Mary Lee Fitzhugh in 1804 and had a daughter, Mary Anna, in 1808. Custis spent many happy years at home with his family. He

The Morning Room in Arlington House, once used by George Washington Parke Custis as a painting studio.

painted scenes from the Revolutionary War based on what George Washington had described to him, and he wrote plays about American history. One, *Pocahontas*, told the story of the early English settlers and Indians in Virginia.

Mrs. Custis was also very busy at Arlington House. She made sure that the house was al-

Mrs. Custis's rose garden.

ways in good shape for visitors. She planted a
rose garden beside their home, which she called
"a very showy handsome building."

When Mary Anna Custis grew up, many
young men wished to marry her. She liked one
better than all the rest, and in 1830 she had
some happy news to share. "Never was I more
surrounded with the joys of life than at this

time," she wrote to a friend. "I am engaged to one to whom I have been long attached—Robert Lee." Dark-haired Robert E. Lee was a lieutenant in the United States Army. He and Mary Anna married in 1831 and made their home at Arlington House.

Over the years, Robert E. Lee's army career often called him away from Arlington House. He went to Missouri to supervise army engineers who were building a harbor in St. Louis. He fought bravely when the United States went to war with Mexico in 1846. After the United States won that war, Lee's commanding officer, General Winfield Scott, called him "the very best soldier that I ever saw in the field."

In 1857, George Washington Parke Custis died. His daughter, Mary Lee, became the owner of Arlington House and the George Washington collection.

The Civil War began a few years later, in 1861, and Robert E. Lee faced a difficult decision. Southern states were seceding, or breaking away, from the United States. One important reason for this was that the Northern states wanted to outlaw slavery but the South didn't. President Abraham Lincoln asked Lee to command the Union army, the fighting force of the Northern states, in the war to reunite the nation.

Lee did not think that states should secede, but he knew that his beloved home state, Virginia, was about to break away. Commanding the Union army would mean fighting against his friends, his loved ones, and his home. Lee could not do that. After a long, sleepless night, he resigned from the U.S. Army to fight for Virginia.

"Lee, you have made the greatest mistake of your life," warned General Scott, Lee's old commander. But Lee would not change his mind. He left Arlington in April 1861. In time, he commanded all of the Confederate, or Southern, forces. He did not know that he would never call Arlington home again.

The rest of the family soon left Arlington, too. They feared that its location, so close to Washington, D.C.—the Northern capital—was unsafe. The family stayed with relatives who lived farther away from the capital. Unfortunately, in their haste to leave, they left behind the George Washington collection.

The Union army crossed the Potomac a short time later and set up its headquarters in Arlington House. While the army built forts on the estate, soldiers looking for souvenirs stole many of the items in the George Washington collection.

In 1862, two things happened that changed Arlington forever. First, Mary Anna Lee, who had become very ill, did not pay her taxes. The United States government claimed her property for its own. Second, President Lincoln freed the slaves in Washington, D.C. These people, along

The Union army set up its headquarters in Arlington House during the Civil War.

with many other freed slaves who had traveled to the capital seeking safety, were called *contrabands*. They had nowhere to live, so the government set up a camp for them, called Freedman's Village, at Arlington. Most would stay until they found jobs or other places to live.

At the same time, bloody battles raged in the countryside around Washington and Arlington.

Many freed slaves lived in Freedman's Village—a camp at Arlington—until they were able to find jobs and homes of their own.

Day after day, the army transported wounded soldiers to hospitals that had been set up quickly in the Union capital. Many of the wounded died in these dirty hospitals—so many that by 1864, the army had filled its cemeteries in Washington and nearby Alexandria, Virginia.

The army's leaders gave Brigadier General Montgomery Meigs the job of finding more cemetery space. To Meigs, Robert E. Lee was a traitor. He suggested burying dead soldiers in the hillsides around Lee's home. That way, thought Meigs, when the war was over the Lee family would never want to live there again. Meigs said that it would be a just punishment for someone who had fought against his own country!

On June 15, 1864, the Union government declared Arlington a national cemetery and began burying the dead. The remains of 2,111 soldiers from nearby battlefields could not be identified. Still General Meigs wanted to give them a military funeral. He ordered a large vault built in the middle of Mrs. Custis's rose garden, and he laid their remains to rest inside it. That vault, now called the Tomb of the Unknown Dead of the Civil War, still stands in the garden near Arlington House.

In 1865, General Lee's Confederate army surrendered. The North and South were reunited, and the people began to reconstruct the

Tomb of the Unknown Dead of the Civil War.

country. It would take years, though, to heal the bitterness and anger between Northerners and Southerners. Almost every American knew someone who had been killed during the war. Many people had lost their homes. Among the refugees were two thousand freed African-Americans who settled in Freedman's Village at Arlington. Robert E. Lee didn't try to regain his estate, but he moved his family to Lexington, Virginia, and became president of Washington College. He wanted the nation to become strong again.

Many people could not forget the thousands of soldiers who had died during the Civil War. General John Alexander Logan, leader of the Grand Army of the Republic, a veterans group, wanted to honor those who had fallen in battle. In 1868, Logan declared that May 30 was to be a special day for remembering "comrades who died in the defense of their country." Americans from the North and South gathered at Arlington National Cemetery on that day to attend religious services and decorate soldiers' graves with flowers. In the years that followed, people throughout the United States observed this day of remembrance, which came to be known as Memorial Day. In 1971, most states began to observe Memorial Day on the last Monday in May.

Memorial Day wasn't the only time that

Americans visited Arlington. People came throughout the year to lay flowers at their loved ones' gravesites. By 1890, most of the inhabitants of Freedman's Village had found permanent homes, and the village was torn down. The land became part of the national cemetery. Around this time, Congress voted to build memorials to people and events in history on Arlington's grounds.

To honor the soldiers who had fought during the Revolutionary War, the remains of eleven men who had died in battle against the British were reburied at Arlington. By the early twentieth century, construction for other memorials was underway.

The place that George Washington Parke Custis created as a tribute to one great American, George Washington, had become a shrine to an entire nation.

ARLINGTON'S MONUMENTS

Wearing a crisp uniform and holding a rifle against his shoulder, a soldier marches twenty-one steps—no more, and no less. The number twenty-one is a symbol of the nation's highest military honor.

This soldier—a member of the United States Third Infantry—guards the Tomb of the Unknowns, Arlington Cemetery's most famous memorial. On behalf of all Americans, he honors the four unknown soldiers buried at this site. Each died in a different twentieth-century war: World War I, World War II, the Korean War, and the Vietnam War. The four unknowns are a symbol, too. They represent all Americans who died in battles throughout the world.

A soldier guards the Tomb of the Unknowns.

    The soldier turns to his left and faces the tomb for twenty-one seconds. The words carved into the marble slab in front of him read: "Here rests in honored glory an American soldier known but to God." The soldier then turns to the right, pauses twenty-one seconds more, and marches forward.

    The Tomb of the Unknowns is guarded for

twenty-four hours a day. Soldiers have been guarding the Tomb since 1937. Each day, a shift of seven enlisted men, all volunteers from the Third Infantry, takes turns marching in front of the Tomb. During the winter the guard changes every hour. In warmer weather the guard is changed every half hour. To stand guard at this monument is an honor, and only after months of training can a soldier take on this important responsibility.

Like all of the monuments at Arlington National Cemetery, the Tomb of the Unknowns keeps alive a story from American history. It tells of the countless Americans who died in war and of a nation that continues to offer its thanks.

Not far from the Tomb, a ship's mast rises into the sky. It is the U.S.S. *Maine* Memorial, a reminder of a sunken American battleship and a tribute to its crew.

Tragedy struck the U.S.S. *Maine* in 1898.

For three weeks the battleship had been an-chored in Havana Harbor, in Cuba. On February 15, without warning, a huge explosion tore through the battleship. Some crew members escaped as water entered the ship's mangled hull, but 260 men lost their lives. Soon a tall mast sticking out of the water was all that could be seen of the *Maine.*

Americans who heard the news were out-raged. The *Maine* had gone to Cuba to help keep peace as the island struggled for its indepen-dence from Spain. Many people blamed Spain for the explosion, although no one knew the real cause. "Remember the *Maine!*" people cried. Soon the United States entered the Spanish-American War. Civil War veterans—soldiers from both the Union and Confederate armies—fought side by side. Their unity helped win the war quickly.

In 1899, Congress had the dead sailors brought home to Arlington National Cemetery for a full military funeral. Eleven years later, Americans returned to Havana Harbor again. This time, they hoisted the *Maine* up from the bottom of the harbor and brought its mast back to the United States. Government workers raised the mast at Arlington, near the graves of the *Maine*'s crew. They built a structure resembling a battleship's turret around the mast and carved the crew members' names in the turret's sides. (A turret is a round structure on which a ship's guns are mounted.) The monument was dedicated in 1912.

Two years later, another monument was unveiled. It was a memorial to the Confederate soldiers who had died during the Civil War. This monument was sponsored by a women's organization called the United Daughters of the Confederacy. They had asked Congress to allow the Confederate soldiers buried throughout Arlington to be brought together in one section of the cemetery. Workers moved Confederate dead

The Confederate Monument.

from other burial grounds to Arlington as well.
The Confederate soldiers' tombstones all have
pointed tops.

   The pointed tombstones circle a carved stone
structure called the Confederate Monument. At
the top of this structure stands a tall, robed
figure representing the South. She holds out a
wreath of laurel, a symbol of honor, to the fallen

Confederates. As a poem carved in the monument explains, these men had not set out to do something wrong. Instead, they had behaved like soldiers everywhere:

...in simple
Obedience to duty
As they understood it
These men suffered all
Sacrificed all
Dared all—and died.

Another memorial tells a more recent story, one that many young people remember. On January 28, 1986, children in schools across the country crowded around television sets to watch the space shuttle *Challenger* take off. Some had seen liftoffs before, but this one was different. A high-school teacher from New Hampshire, Christa McAuliffe, was going along, too. She had been chosen from among the thousands of teachers who had applied to go. To prepare for the trip Christa underwent extensive training, just like the astronauts.

Suddenly, as America watched, the *Challenger* broke apart in flames. Pieces of the space shuttle tumbled to the ocean, and McAuliffe and the other astronauts on board lost their lives.

Finding the bodies took weeks. Sadly, not all of the remains could be identified. The government returned those that were identified to the astronauts' families. Some families buried their loved ones near their home. Christa McAuliffe was buried near her family's home in Concord, New Hampshire. Two of the astronauts, Francis R. "Dick" Scobee and Michael J. Smith, were buried at Arlington. Each had had a long military career and had earned medals for bravery in the war in Vietnam.

The rest of the remains—those never identified—were placed in a grave near their fellow astronauts, Scobee and Smith. Fourteen months after the accident, on a clear, windy March day in 1987, a special ceremony was held at the site. George Bush, then the vice president, unveiled the 6 foot (1.82-meter) *Challenger* Memorial that stands above those remains. "Progress sometimes extracts a terrible toll," Bush said. But he assured those present that the accident would not stop America's experiments in space. "We will complete the great voyage," he promised.

A large bronze plaque on the *Challenger* Memorial displays portraits of the seven astronauts. Many visitors recognize them from television and newspaper reports. Often monuments are made to look larger than life. These seven portraits show visitors that the accident wasn't just a technological disaster but a human one. It also reminds visitors that those striving to accomplish great things are people who have families just like them. Many of the people buried in Arlington were not as famous as the seven astronauts. Yet they, too, faced danger and death.

Since the Spanish-American War, thousands

The Challenger *Memorial.*

of nurses have braved the hazards of battle to care for wounded soldiers. While helping others, some of the nurses lost their own lives. Arlington's Nurses Memorial honors their courage and hard work. At the top of a slope, a tall, sculpted woman in a nurse's cape stands watching over the graves of Army, Navy, and Air Force nurses.

Many Americans served with courage in the Coast Guard, too. The United States Coast Guard Memorial thanks all of the Coast Guard personnel who have worked to protect people's lives and property at sea. The base of the monument—a sturdy stone pyramid—stands for the Coast Guard's steady strength. Attached to the pyramid is a bronze sea gull. Like the Coast Guard, the sea gull seems to be carefully scanning the surface of the sea.

When enemy torpedoes sank two Coast Guard ships during World War I—killing all of the officers and crew on board—the American public reacted with sorrow. The Coast Guard

Memorial, which was dedicated in 1928, expresses that grief. Carved in the monument are the names of all who died aboard the *Seneca* and the *Tampa,* the two sunken ships, as well as the other Coast Guard members who died in World War I.

American history is a story about people. Any time the nation has gone to war, soldiers have fought and died, while families have worried and mourned. During times of peace many soldiers have gone on to become famous scientists, actors, athletes, politicians, and astronauts. The memorials at Arlington National Cemetery honor all of these people, from the unknown soldiers to the presidents. Each monument tells the story of a great man or woman and what he or she did to improve America.

The United States Coast Guard Memorial.

CHAPTER 4

FAMOUS IN LIFE

On November 22, 1963, President John F. Kennedy visited Dallas, Texas. As he rode in an open car past a crowd of waving Texans, he was suddenly struck by rifle bullets and fell over in his seat. The driver of the car rushed the president to a nearby hospital, but the doctors could not help. Quickly, the news spread throughout the world that President Kennedy was dead.

Many Americans felt shocked and saddened by the death of President Kennedy, a leader who had made them proud. This man had traveled all over the world, trying to promote friendship between the United States and other nations. He had formed the Peace Corps, which sent American volunteers to other countries in need of aid. The volunteers lived among the people of those countries, teaching them ways to improve their farming, communities, and health. He had been a strong supporter of the civil rights movement, and he introduced the first Civil Rights Act in Congress.

John F. Kennedy had been a war hero, too. As a navy lieutenant during World War II, he commanded the torpedo boat *PT-109*. He risked his own life to save his crew after a Japanese destroyer collided with their ship and broke it in two.

On November 25, 1963, a horse-drawn wagon carried the president's body across Arlington's Memorial Bridge. Eight servicemen lowered Kennedy's casket into a hillside grave near Arlington House. Twenty-one guns fired a final salute, and fifty-one planes flew overhead. The planes stood for the fifty states and the leader they had lost. Jacqueline Kennedy, the president's widow, stepped forward to light the

An Eternal Flame will burn forever at President John F. Kennedy's grave.

Eternal Flame. The light of this flame will burn forever. Through this, the memory of the president and what he accomplished remains alive.

Near John Kennedy's burial site, a simple white cross marks the grave of his brother,

A large crowd visits John F. Kennedy's hillside grave near Arlington House.

Robert F. Kennedy. Robert Kennedy served as U.S. attorney general from 1961 until 1964 and then became a United States senator. In both jobs, he worked to make life better for many Americans. He helped to end segregation (the separation of blacks and whites) in many Southern schools, and he brought financial and social help to poor people in inner-city neighborhoods.

He also fought hard against organized crime.

Robert Kennedy was hoping to run for president in 1968. On June 5, after giving a speech to a cheering crowd in California, he, too, was hit by an assassin's bullet. He died the next day.

Just northeast of the Kennedys' graves, shade trees overlook a tall granite monument. It marks the graves of President William Howard Taft and his wife, Helen Herron Taft. Taft lived in the White House from 1909 until 1913. He called it "the lonesomest place in the world."

Many of Taft's policies were unpopular, but he accomplished some important things while president. For example, he helped to break up several trusts—powerful businesses that controlled prices and supplies. In 1921, Taft became chief justice of the Supreme Court, the highest position in the government's justice system. He liked being a justice much more than he liked being a president, and he wrote, "I don't remember that I ever was president."

President William Howard Taft.

Two other chief justices, Oliver Wendell Holmes, Jr., and Earl Warren, are also buried at Arlington. Holmes, wounded in the Civil War, was a Supreme Court justice for twenty-nine years. He retired in 1932 at age ninety. Two years later, President Franklin Roosevelt asked him why, at age ninety-two, he was reading difficult works by ancient Greek authors. "To improve my mind, Mr. President," Holmes answered quickly. Warren, who became chief justice in 1953, helped to decide important court cases dealing with civil rights. He is also remembered as the head of the Warren Commission. This group investigated President Kennedy's assassination. Both Holmes and Warren were dedicated to ensuring justice to all Americans.

Another man who defended Americans' freedom was General Omar Bradley. One of Arlington's tombstones marks his grave. Bradley led the Americans and their allies across Europe during World War II. Admiral William F. Halsey, another World War II hero, is also buried at Arlington. Under the command of stocky "Bull" Halsey, the United States Navy battled the Japanese in the South Pacific. The navy sank Japanese ships, shot down many planes, and destroyed fuel supplies.

One of World War II's best-known heroes was Audie Murphy, son of a poor Texas farmer.

While Murphy was commanding an army unit in France, his men came under German attack. Murphy jumped onto a burning tank destroyer and began to fire his machine gun. He kept shooting for an hour, even after being wounded in the leg. It was this man's bravery that held back the German tanks and soldiers. He received more medals than any other soldier in World War II, and his picture appeared on magazine covers. After the war, he became a movie actor and starred in more than forty films. One, *To Hell and Back*, told of his wartime experiences. Another, *The Red Badge of Courage*, showed a Civil War soldier's first reaction to battle.

Like the tombstones of other military personnel at Arlington, Murphy's lists the medals that he received. It tells visitors in which war he fought and the military rank that he achieved.

Many famous people buried at Arlington served in the military but are better known for

Astronauts (bottom to top) *Gus Grissom, Edward White, and Roger Chaffee. Grissom and Chaffee are buried at Arlington.*

other achievements. Among them are astronauts Gus Grissom and Roger Chaffee. Both men worked hard for America's space program. They believed that exploration of the universe would help humans understand themselves better. On January 27, 1967, they sat in their Apollo One spacecraft preparing for a fourteen-day trip into space. Suddenly, sparks flew from a faulty wire onto one of their controls. Fire spread quickly through the craft, killing Grissom, Chaffee, and Ed White, the third crew member. Grissom and Chaffee were buried side by side at Arlington. White lies in the cemetery at the U.S. Military Academy at West Point, where he had been a student years before.

Medgar Evers, who is also buried at Arlington, was an important civil rights worker. In 1963, Evers, a World War II veteran, was working with the National Association for the Advancement of Colored People (NAACP) in Mississippi. He had had a chance to work at the NAACP's headquarters in New York but refused it. He wanted to stay in Mississippi and help end segregation in the South. "The fight is here," he said.

On June 12, Evers heard President Kennedy speak on television about civil rights. The speech called for equal treatment of all Americans. That night, Evers spoke to a crowd gathered at a Mississippi church on that some topic. Most of those present agreed with Evers that segregation must end. Evers's words angered some white Southerners in the audience, though. As he returned home that night he was shot to death. Evers became a symbol of courage and sacrifice in the struggle for equal treatment of blacks.

Another famous black American buried at Arlington is Joe Louis. As boxing's world heavyweight champion from 1937 until 1949, Louis gained the love and respect of many Americans. In 1938, seventy thousand people came to see him win "the fight of the century" against Max Schmeling of Germany. Just a few years later, the United States and its allies would be fighting against Germany and Japan in World War II. Joe Louis enlisted as a regular soldier, but to the troops he was already a hero. To help take the men's minds off of the horror of war, Joe Louis fought in ninety-six specially arranged matches at different army bases overseas. Joe

Louis's tombstone displays a portrait of the famous fighter in his boxing gloves and trunks, along with his nickname, "The Brown Bomber."

The achievements of the well-known people buried at Arlington are many. Walter Reed discovered how to prevent yellow fever, a serious disease carried by mosquitoes in tropical climates. George Westinghouse invented an air brake for railroad trains and a safe way to pipe natural gas into houses. Robert Peary and Matthew Henson became the first explorers to reach the North Pole. All of these people used their lives to make the world a better place. At Arlington, Americans honor them and silently say "Thanks."

CHAPTER 5

AMERICA REMEMBERS

Clouds cover the sky at Arlington National Cemetery on the last Monday in May. Tiny raindrops fall on the crowd that has gathered this morning. Twenty-one times, the boom of a cannon rumbles over the cemetery's hills, as the vice president of the United States places a wreath of flowers at the Tomb of the Unknowns. It is Memorial Day, the day when Americans honor the men and women killed in wartime. The vice president has joined his fellow citizens to remember the heroic dead.

Americans fill every seat in the Memorial Amphitheater, located just north of the Tomb of the Unknowns. Others crowd together at the rear or stand outside, hoping to see—or at least

The Memorial Amphitheater.

to hear—the Memorial Day service. Large
American flags hang between each of the amphitheater's white marble columns.

As the U.S. Army Band plays, uniformed
veterans march into the arena. The crowd
stands to recite the Pledge of Allegiance and
sing "The Star-Spangled Banner." Then Colonel
John Morrison, Arlington Cemetery's staff chap-

A man prepares to place flowers on a loved one's grave.

lain, prays for the many Americans who have sacrificed their lives to protect people's freedom.

Colorful, fragrant wreaths of flowers decorate the U.S.S. *Maine* Memorial, the Confederate Monument, and other memorials. Many families place flowers on the graves of loved ones. Some find the gravesites easily, while others rely on maps and instructions from the cemetery's Visitors' Center. The Visitors' Center also provides them with passes so that they may bring their cars into the cemetery. People with passes are the only visitors who may drive on Arlington's eighteen miles of roads.

Beyond the Memorial Amphitheater, visitors see small flags everywhere. For this day of remembrance, the army has marked each of Arlington's 219,000 graves with an American flag. There is a flag on the grave of Private William Christman, the first Union soldier buried at Arlington during the Civil War. Identical flags stand on the graves of soldiers who died in America's most recent conflicts—in Panama and the Middle East.

Those visitors who wish to see Arlington's other sights may travel on foot or ride in shuttle buses. The buses stop at the Tomb of the Unknowns, the Kennedys' graves, and Arlington House. Tour guides aboard these buses point out sites of interest and explain aspects of Arlington's history. A staff of historians is constantly researching the stories of the many heroes buried at the cemetery.

The visitors who stop at John F. Kennedy's grave see a flag there, too. They also see the Eternal Flame in the patch of fieldstone that covers Kennedy's grave. The fieldstone comes from Cape Cod, Massachusetts, one of President Kennedy's favorite places. Buried beside President Kennedy are two of his children, a girl and a boy who died as infants. Flags mark their graves, too, and magnolia trees shade the area. There are more than seventeen thousand trees on Arlington's grounds.

Another popular stop is Arlington House, a memorial to Robert E. Lee. As visitors tour the house, they see the bedrooms where the Lee family slept and the Morning Room, where George Washington Parke Custis painted and wrote his plays. Custis's large painting of George Washington on horseback stands in the corner of this room. Guides dressed in costumes of the early 1800s answer any questions that visitors might have.

Outside Arlington House, flags decorate the graves of Custis and his wife, located in the small, fenced-in family burial ground. On the hillside below, flags mark the graves of Robert Kennedy and William Howard Taft, Medgar Evers and Walter Reed. Flags decorate every gravestone in the Nurses Section and on Chaplains' Hill, where members of the clergy—priests, ministers, and rabbis—are buried. Of different religious faiths, these men brought comfort to wartime troops far from home.

Flags also stand in front of tombstones marking empty graves. This section of the cemetery is in memory of people who died in war but whose bodies were never found. The tombstones in the memorial sections give these heroes the honor that they have earned.

On Memorial Day, flags decorate the graves

in a large, older section of Arlington Cemetery, too. This was the burial ground for many freed and escaped slaves who died in Freedman's Village and in other settlement camps in the Washington, D.C., area. Each of these graves is simply marked with the name of the man, woman, or child buried there and often the single word "Citizen."

Everyone buried at Arlington Cemetery played a part in American history. Many worked hard and faced danger to protect the freedom of Americans and others throughout the world. A visit to Arlington National Cemetery is a chance to learn about events in history. It is an opportunity to remember those events and the people who took part in them. Arlington National Cemetery is a place for giving thanks—not just on Memorial Day but on every day of the year.

On Memorial Day, an American flag marks each of Arlington's 219,000 graves.

Burial at Arlington National Cemetery

Burial at Arlington National Cemetery is permitted for the following members of the military service:

★ Those who died on active duty.

★ Those who served for twenty years or more.

★ Veterans who suffered 30 percent or more disability and were honorably discharged from the military before October 1, 1949.

★ Men and women who have received any of these military decorations: The Medal of Honor, Distinguished Service Cross, Air Force Cross, Navy Cross, Distinguished Service Medal, Silver Star, or Purple Heart.

★ Presidents of the United States. (The president is considered commander-in-chief of all of the military forces.)

★ Members of the president's cabinet, other nationally elected officials, and Supreme Court justices who served honorably in the military.

The husbands and wives of those people, as well as their unmarried children under age twenty-one, may also be buried at Arlington. Also, the president or secretary of the army can give special permission to allow others to be buried at Arlington National Cemetery.

Veterans who were honorably discharged from military service but do not fit into one of the categories for burial may be *inurned* at Arlington—they may have their ashes buried at the cemetery following cremation. Their spouses and dependent children may also be inurned.

WELL-KNOWN PEOPLE BURIED AT ARLINGTON NATIONAL CEMETERY

Henry "Hap" Arnold   1886-1950   Army and air force general; carried the first air-mail shipments in 1911; pioneered airborne patrolling of forest fires.

Constance Bennett   1904-1965   Actress who starred in plays and movies; wife of air force colonel John Coulter.

Omar N. Bradley   1893-1981   Army general; led the American invasion of Europe in World War II.

Richard E. Byrd, Jr.   1888-1957   Discovered new regions, mountain ranges, and bodies of water in Antarctica.

Roger Chaffee   1935-1967   Apollo I astronaut.

Abner Doubleday   1819-1893   Civil War hero; organized many baseball teams as a young man; established the rules of that game.

Medgar Evers   1925-1963   Civil rights worker.

Virgil I. "Gus" Grissom   1926-1967   Apollo I astronaut.

Dashiell Hammett   1894-1961   Author of *The Maltese Falcon, The Thin Man,* and other detective novels; veteran of World War I and World War II.

Matthew Henson   1866-1955   One of the first explorers to reach the North Pole.

Daniel "Chappie" James, Jr.   1920-1978   The first African-American to achieve the rank of four-star general— the second-highest rank in the air force or army.

John F. Kennedy   1917-1963   President of the United States; World War II veteran.

Robert F. Kennedy   1925-1968   Attorney general under President John F. Kennedy; United States senator from New York.

Pierre Charles L'Enfant   1754-1825   Revolutionary War veteran; planned the layout of streets and location of government buildings in Washington, D.C.

Robert Todd Lincoln   1843-1926   Secretary of war under presidents James Garfield and Chester A. Arthur; son of President Abraham Lincoln.

Joe Louis   1914-1981   Boxing's former heavyweight champion of the world.

George C. Marshall   1880-1959   Army general; secretary of state under President Harry S. Truman; won the Nobel Peace Prize in 1953 for developing the Marshall Plan, a program for rebuilding Europe after World War II.

Lee Marvin   1924-1987   Movie actor; won the Academy Award for best actor in 1965 for his role in *Cat Ballou*; received the Purple Heart, which is awarded to military personnel wounded in combat.

Anita Newcomb McGee   1864-1940   The army's first woman surgeon.

Montgomery Meigs   1816-1892   Civil War general; chose the site of Arlington National Cemetery.

Audie Murphy   1924-1971   Most decorated soldier of World War II; movie actor.

Robert E. Peary   1856-1920   Led the first group of explorers to reach the North Pole.

Walter Reed   1851-1902   Discovered how to prevent and control yellow fever.

Francis R. "Dick" Scobee   1939-1986   Space shuttle *Challenger* astronaut.

Michael J. Smith   1945-1986   Space shuttle *Challenger* astronaut.

William Howard Taft   1857-1930   President of the United States; chief justice of the Supreme Court.

George Westinghouse   1846-1914   Credited with many inventions, including air brakes for railroad trains.

Arlington's Major Monuments and Memorials

Confederate Monument—A memorial to the soldiers who died fighting for the Confederacy during the Civil War. A female figure (representing the South) offers a laurel wreath—a symbol of honor—to the Confederate soldiers buried at Arlington.

Nurses Memorial—A female figure, carved from stone, dedicated to the memory of army, navy, and air force nurses who served in war.

101st Army Airborne Division Memorial—A bronze statue of an eagle about to take flight sits at the top of this memorial. It symbolizes the 101st Airborne Division—known as the "Screaming Eagles"—which fought in World War II and Vietnam.

Rough Riders Memorial—A dark gray stone pillar bearing the insignia of the First U.S. Volunteer Cavalry, known as the "Rough Riders." Led by Theodore Roosevelt, the Rough Riders participated in the battle of San Juan Hill in Cuba during the Spanish-American War. The memorial also bears the names of Rough Riders who died during that war.

Seabees Memorial—Erected in memory of the U.S. Naval Construction Battalion, known as the "Seabees," which built military bases in Europe and the Pacific during World War II. A statue of a Seabee making friends with a child stands before a large carving of Seabees at work.

Tomb of the Unknown Dead of the Civil War—A vault that contains the remains of 2,111 Civil War soldiers who died on or near the battlefield of Bull Run (Manassas), Virginia. These soldiers stand for everyone who died in the Civil War and could not be identified.

Tomb of the Unknown Dead of the War of 1812—A granite slab marks the gravesite of fourteen unknown soldiers from the War of 1812. The United States fought England in that war to protect the rights of American ships upon the seas. The battles took place along the eastern coast of Canada and the United States. The fourteen unknowns are symbolic of all Americans who died in that war.

Tomb of the Unknowns—A marble tomb holds the remains of four unknown soldiers, one who died in World War I, one in World War II, another in the Korean War, and the last in the Vietnam War. The four represent all Americans who have ever died in war.

United States Coast Guard Memorial—A bronze sea gull—the symbol of the Coast Guard—appears to fly in front of a stone pyramid. The memorial honors all Coast Guard members who have died in the line of duty.

United States Marine Corps Memorial—A bronze statue of six Marines raising the American flag on the island of Iwo Jima during World War II. This monument was erected in memory of all Marines who have died in war.

U.S.S. *Maine* Memorial—The mast of the U.S.S. *Maine*, which sank in Havana Harbor at the start of the Spanish-American War. The monument's base resembles a battleship's turret.

War Correspondents Memorial—A tree grows as a living memorial to all news reporters who died while bringing information about wars to the American public.

ARLINGTON NATIONAL CEMETERY: A HISTORICAL TIME LINE

1802 George Washington Parke Custis begins to build a home and memorial to George Washington on the land that his natural father purchased.

1831 Mary Anna Custis marries Second Lieutenant Robert E. Lee.

1861 The Civil War begins; Robert E. Lee resigns from the United States Army to fight for Virginia; the Lee family flees Arlington House; the Union army establishes its headquarters at Arlington House.

1862 Mary Anna Lee fails to pay the taxes on her Arlington estate; the United States government claims the property; President Abraham Lincoln frees the slaves in the District of Columbia.

1864 Arlington becomes a military cemetery.

1868 Americans observe the first Memorial Day at Arlington National Cemetery.

1912 The mast of the U.S.S. *Maine* is placed at Arlington National Cemetery.

1920 Arlington's Memorial Amphitheater is dedicated.

1921 An unknown soldier from World War I is buried in the Tomb of the Unknowns.

1958 Unknown soldiers from World War II and the Korean War are buried in the Tomb of the Unknowns.

1963 President John F. Kennedy is assassinated in Dallas, Texas, and buried at Arlington National Cemetery.

1984 An unknown soldier from the Vietnam War is buried in the Tomb of the Unknowns.

1987 Vice President George Bush unveils the memorial to the seven *Challenger* astronauts at Arlington National Cemetery.

Visitor Information

Hours
8:00 A.M. to 7:00 P.M., April through September
8:00 A.M. to 5:00 P.M., October through March

Tours
Narrated shuttle service is available for a fee; stops at the Tomb of the Unknowns, the Kennedy gravesites, and Arlington House.

Special Events
The Memorial Day and Veterans Day services are held at 11:00 A.M. in the Memorial Amphitheater; the Easter Service is held at sunrise in the Memorial Amphitheater.

Arlington House
Open from 9:30 A.M. until 6:00 P.M. from April through September, and from 9:30 A.M. until 4:30 P.M. from October through March; brochures are available for a self-guided walking tour; interpreters in period costumes answer visitors' questions.

Visitors Center
Provides maps, general information, and help in finding specific gravesites; issues passes to people wishing to drive to a family member's grave; site of the tourmobile office, bookstore, and rest rooms.

Additional information can be obtained from:

Arlington National Cemetery
Arlington, VA 22211
(703) 692-0931

Arlington House
George Washington Memorial Parkway
Turkey Run Park
McLean, VA 22101
(703) 557-0613

Index

72